BBC
DOCTOR WHO
Face the Raven

A story based on the original script by
SARAH DOLLARD

Level 3

Retold by Nancy Taylor

Series Editors: Andy Hopkins and Jocelyn Potter

T0352432

Pearson Education Limited
KAO Two
KAO Park, Harlow,
Essex, CM17 9NA, England
and Associated Companies throughout the world.

ISBN: 978-1-292-20619-6
This edition first published by Pearson Education Ltd 2018
5 7 9 10 8 6

BBC, DOCTOR WHO (word marks, logos and devices), TARDIS, DALEKS, CYBERMAN
and K-9 (word marks and devices) are trade marks of the British Broadcasting
Corporation and are used under licence. BBC logo © BBC 1996. Doctor Who logo © BBC
2009. Licensed by BBC Worldwide Limited.

The authors have asserted their moral rights in accordance
with the Copyright Designs and Patents Act 1988
Set in 9pt/14pt Xenois Slab Pro
Printed in China
SWTC/05

All rights reserved; no part of this publication may be reproduced,
stored in a retrieval system, or transmitted in any form or by any means, electronic,
mechanical, photocopying, recording, or otherwise, without the prior written
permission of the Publishers.

Published by Pearson Education Limited

For a complete list of the titles available in the Pearson English Readers series, visit
www.pearsonenglishreaders.com.
Alternatively, write to your local Pearson Education office or
to Pearson English Readers Marketing Department,
Pearson Education, KAO Two, KAO Park, Harlow, Essex, CM17 9NA

Contents

The Doctor

The Doctor is an alien, a Time Lord from Gallifrey, far away in a different world. He travels through time and space, has adventures and saves people in danger. He has two hearts, and he is about 2,000 years old. When the Doctor's body becomes old or ill, he changes it for a new one. He has had many different bodies before the one in this story. The Doctor doesn't use a gun, and tries not to kill anyone. But he does have other tools which help him in his adventures. With his sonic sunglasses, for example, the Doctor can see important information that humans cannot see. In many ways, he seems like an alien from a science fiction story. But he is also a very kind, funny and loving person with a wonderful imagination.

The TARDIS

The Doctor travels through time and space in a time machine called the TARDIS. On the outside, the TARDIS looks like a blue police box from Earth. These blue boxes were used in the UK, many years ago, to call the police. The inside of the TARDIS is very different and, surprisingly, much bigger. It has many rooms full of computers and other electronic equipment.

The Doctor's Companion: Clara Oswald

The Doctor usually travels with someone from Earth. His companion is his assistant and friend and helps him on his adventures. At the end of an adventure, the TARDIS returns the companion to Earth. They usually arrive back at exactly the same time as they left. In this story, the Doctor's companion is Clara Oswald, an English teacher at a London school.

Rigsy

Rigsy is a young graffiti artist who has helped the Doctor and Clara in the past. He lives in central London with Jen and their baby, Lucy.

Ashildr ('Madam Mayor')

Ashildr has lived for more than 1000 years, since the Doctor made her immortal. He saved her life, but she isn't always grateful. She has had many adventures and has forgotten a lot of them. She remembers by reading her diaries. She is now the mayor of a hidden street of aliens.

Anah and Anahson

Anah and her child Anahson live on the hidden street. They are Janus, aliens with two faces – one at the front and one at the back of their heads. Females like Anah can see into the future and back into the past.

Rump and Kabel

Rump is an alien who lives on the hidden street. He and Kabel work for Ashildr. Rump is Kabel's boss.

Introduction

'We don't punish criminals with an easy death. He broke the law. He has to face the raven,' Ashildr said coldly.

The Doctor, Clara and Rigsy are on an unknown street in central London. Ordinary British people know nothing about this street and never notice it. The population of this hidden street are aliens. They live peacefully, unseen by ordinary humans. But the Doctor and Clara needed to find the street because Rigsy is in trouble with the aliens there. These aliens have decided that Rigsy is a murderer. Their law says that he must face the raven. He must die.

The Doctor and Clara are sure that their friend, Rigsy, is not guilty of murder. But how can they prove this to the aliens and to their leader, Ashildr? Will any of them leave the street alive? Or will each of them have to face the raven?

Doctor Who first appeared on British television in 1963 in black and white. It was a great success, with its new electronic sounds and crazy stories in space. The programmes were shown until 1989. Years later, *Doctor Who* returned with a new writing team. The stories became funnier and more adult, but the central idea is the same. The Doctor travels through space in the TARDIS, his time machine, helping people in their fights with aliens. These programmes are very popular in many countries around the world.

Peter Capaldi plays the Twelfth Doctor. The Doctor always has the same history, but each actor brings something new to the part. Capaldi has always loved *Doctor Who*. When he went into the TARDIS for the first time, he felt at home. 'I know how to work the TARDIS,' he said. 'I've known for a long time.'

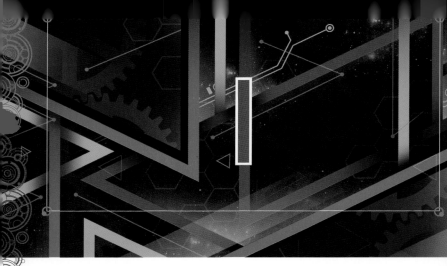

The Mysterious Tattoo

The door to the TARDIS crashed open and the Doctor and Clara hurried inside. They were both laughing so hard that they almost fell over.

'Oh! I'm glad to see the TARDIS!' shouted Clara. She jumped into the air, feeling very pleased with herself. 'That was the best escape ever! My plan worked!'

'That alien nearly ate you for dinner, Clara,' said the Doctor, as he tried to clean something like alien soup from his clothes.

'Our stories are a little different, Doctor,' Clara laughed. 'Think again. Don't you remember? I saved your life.'

'That thing couldn't kill me!' the Doctor shouted.

'I saved you from marriage to a very large plant,' Clara replied. 'And you couldn't believe our luck when we escaped. It was exciting, wasn't it?'

The Doctor smiled. 'You're right. It was wonderful, and I was amused by the possibility of marriage. Imagine that!'

'Ha! I knew you were surprised!' Clara said happily.

The TARDIS phone rang. Clara and the Doctor both looked worried. Nobody ever called them on this phone.

The Doctor told Clara to answer it.

'Hello?' Clara said quietly.

'Clara? Finally. It's Rigsy,' a voice said.

'Oh, Rigsy! Hi! What's wrong?' Clara asked.

Rigsy was phoning from his flat in central London. He was standing in front of the bathroom mirror. He was feeling nervous as he looked carefully at the back of his neck.

'Clara, I don't know what to do. I have this thing on the back of my neck. It looks like a tattoo. But it can't be. I'm not sure what it is.'

'Are you joking?' asked Clara. 'I gave you this number for serious problems. *Very* serious problems.'

'Clara, this is serious, believe me. Come here and look at it. Please!' Rigsy asked.

The Doctor looked unhappy and spoke quietly to Clara. 'Why does someone have my phone number? I told you not to give it to anyone. It's against the rules!'

Clara waved the Doctor away and spoke to Rigsy. 'Listen. We can't take you back in time to stop you getting a tattoo. Can't you live with it?'

'You don't understand,' Rigsy said. 'I didn't *get* a tattoo. I didn't *ask* for it. I woke up this morning and it was there. It's a number. I think that it's

'I have this thing on the back of my neck. It looks like a tattoo. But it can't be. I'm not sure what it is.'

counting down to zero. The number changes every minute.'

'What are you talking about? That doesn't make any sense,' Clara said.

Rigsy looked at his neck in the mirror. 'I'm watching the tattoo now. The number's just changed from 537 to 536. What does it mean? Can you help me?'

'That sounds serious,' Clara agreed. 'We're on our way.'

'Hurry. Please,' Rigsy said.

Clara and the Doctor knew Rigsy from one of their earlier adventures. When they met him, Rigsy was in trouble because of his art. He liked to paint graffiti on places like walls, bridges and trains. The police caught him, and as a punishment he had to help clean the city streets for a few weeks. While he was doing this, people near his flat began to disappear for no reason. With Rigsy's help, the Doctor and Clara solved the mystery, and the three of them became friends.

After that, the Doctor always called Rigsy 'Local Knowledge', because the young man knew London's back streets, its hidden corners and its men and women so well.

The TARDIS arrived at Rigsy's flat and Clara and the Doctor walked out. Rigsy was waiting there, holding his baby daughter.

'Local Knowledge! What's happening?' the Doctor asked. 'And did you make this little person?' The Doctor was interested in babies. Things were different on Gallifrey, and human babies always surprised him.

'Yes – me and Jen. This is my daughter, Lucy,' Rigsy explained.

Lucy looked at the Doctor and Clara and smiled. She was a happy, healthy baby without a worry in the world.

'Oh, she's beautiful,' Clara said, holding Lucy's little hand.

'She's better than that - she's excellent! Forget about tattoos. Stay at home with this new person,' the Doctor told Rigsy. 'Nothing is more

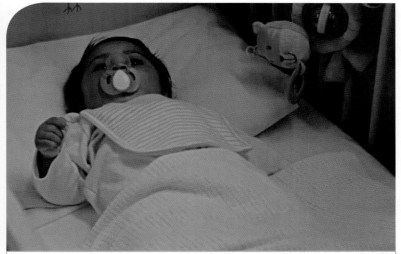

'Local Knowledge! What's happening?' the Doctor asked. 'And did you make this little person?'

important than her.'

'Of course, but listen,' Rigsy began. 'I didn't go out and ask for a tattoo. It was there when I woke up this morning. Jen noticed it before I did.'

'Show me this mysterious tattoo that you didn't ask for,' the Doctor ordered Rigsy.

The young man turned around, and the Doctor looked closely at his neck. The tattoo read 533.

'It's a boring tattoo,' said the Doctor. 'Nothing special.'

'Doctor, please wait. Watch it,' Rigsy said patiently.

'What were you doing last night?' Clara asked Rigsy.

'That's part of my problem,' Rigsy explained. 'I can't remember anything about yesterday. Jen says that I left for work very early. But nobody saw me at work all day. And I didn't come home until after midnight.'

Suddenly, the tattoo changed from 533 to 532. The Doctor was surprised. This was mysterious.

'That's not boring. That's really interesting!' he shouted. He put on his sonic sunglasses and looked at the tattoo more carefully. These glasses were one of the Doctor's most important tools. Because he could see above, below and into things with them, an examination usually produced something surprising.

'That's not possible,' he said, after looking again at the tattoo.

'What's happening?' Clara asked.

'You, Local Knowledge, are coming with us. Bring the new person. No, leave her with her mother,' the Doctor ordered. 'A new person is too interesting to have with us. We have work to do.'

The Doctor, Clara and Rigsy climbed into the TARDIS. They hoped to solve the mystery of Rigsy's tattoo. Clara used a computer program in the TARDIS to check Rigsy's phone. She wanted to find out about the last twenty-four hours of his life. Where did he go? What did he do?

'There's nothing on your phone from yesterday,' she told Rigsy. 'Nothing at all. No messages, no list of calls, no information about where you were. That's really strange.'

At the same time, the Doctor was using special electronic equipment to check Rigsy from head to toe.

'Local Knowledge, don't move while I check you,' he ordered. 'I don't want you to lose an arm or a leg. Or one of each! Ah! I can see that in the past twenty-four hours you have been with aliens. You met them here, in the centre of London. What did they want from you?'

Rigsy was alarmed. He couldn't move - or speak. He looked very worried.

'OK,' the Doctor said. 'You can move now.'

'Thanks! But why don't I remember anything?' asked Rigsy.

'You've been Retconned,' explained the Doctor.

'I've been what?' Rigsy asked.

'What did you say?' Clara asked the Doctor. 'Retconned? What's that?'

'The aliens gave Local Knowledge one of their special drinks. His mind is swimming in it. That's why, Local Knowledge, all your memories of yesterday have disappeared. That's Retconned. Oh, wait. There's more ...' The Doctor checked his computer. 'Very strange. Not good.'

The Doctor looked worried again. He hurried behind Rigsy and checked his neck: 526. He understood now. But he didn't know how to explain things to the young man. He didn't always understand how to be kind to people. Should he tell him or not? He turned his back on Rigsy and made urgent faces at Clara.

Clara realised what was happening. *No. Not Rigsy! He can't die!* she thought.

Rigsy saw the sad, worried look on Clara's face. 'What?' he asked her. 'Tell me. What does the Doctor know?'

'Rigsy, your tattoo – it's called a Chronolock. I'm afraid you're ...' the Doctor began.

Rigsy suddenly looked frightened. 'No, no, no ... don't use my real name!' he shouted. 'Call me Local Knowledge or Tattoo Boy, but don't call me Rigsy. It's serious when you call me that. This is *not* serious. You're going to save me. You're the Doctor. That's what you do.'

Clara looked at the Doctor with a question in her eyes: *Can you save Rigsy?* She didn't want her young friend to know that she was afraid for him. She spoke quietly to the Doctor.

'Doctor, can you explain what a Chronolock is? Then we can get to work.'

'More teaching! It's a simple tool. It's often in the form of a tattoo that looks like a number. But, as we've seen, the number continues to change, minute by minute,' explained the Doctor.

'And what happens when the number on my tattoo – the Chronolock – reaches zero?' Rigsy asked nervously.

'We can talk about that later,' the Doctor told him. 'Now, no more standing around. Let's solve this problem. First, we have to stop the countdown. The tattoo says 526, so we've got 526 minutes. That's less than nine hours. Local Knowledge, I don't know who did this to you. Or why. But maybe I know how to find them. Let's begin!'

A Trap Street

The TARDIS landed outside the British Library, in the middle of London, and the Doctor hurried in through the library's main entrance. Clara and Rigsy followed behind him as quickly as possible.

'Doctor, why are we here?' Clara asked.

'There have always been stories about hidden streets in central London. The stories were talked about in secret and passed from traveller to traveller. And along these streets, you will – they say – find aliens. But first we must find the streets,' the Doctor explained.

'Are these hidden places here, in the British Library?' asked Rigsy. 'Is that possible?'

'No,' the Doctor replied. 'Not the streets – the maps are here. Follow me to the map room.'

In the map room, the Doctor looked at a very old map of London and compared it to a pile of modern maps.

'The idea of hidden streets has never interested me,' the Doctor explained. 'How did London streets suddenly disappear? That didn't seem possible. That seemed careless, even for humans. But if the stories are true, these maps will help us. There should be a street on this old map that doesn't exist on the new maps. But that street still exists somewhere. We just can't see it. I mean, we can't see it on an ordinary day with ordinary eyes.'

'Like a "trap street" – but not,' Clara said. 'I've read about trap streets. They're not real streets. In the past, a map-maker often added a small street that didn't exist. He named it after his wife or one of his children, perhaps. It was like a signature on his work. Then sometimes the trap street appeared on another map-maker's work. The first map-maker knew that somebody was copying his work. Clever, right?'

'We're looking for a trap street? A street that doesn't exist?' asked Rigsy.

'Well, we're looking for a different kind of trap street. A hidden street that aliens use for their own purposes. We're looking for a trap street that *does* exist. But I was wrong. We're not going to find it here,' said the Doctor. 'Let's go back into the TARDIS.'

The TARDIS took the three searchers high into the sky. In a strong wind and with the doors open, Clara lay on her stomach. The top half of her body was hanging out of the time machine. She was searching for one of the mysterious hidden trap streets with the help of the Doctor's sonic sunglasses.

'Don't move around, Clara,' the Doctor told his assistant. 'Be calm and look straight down.'

'I know. I know,' Clara said. 'I'm only looking at the buildings straight under me.'

'The aliens have a way of hiding these streets,' the Doctor explained to Rigsy. 'Our eyes don't see them. With the sonic sunglasses, we can record everything that Clara sees. Then we'll have a map on our computer of what she was looking at. We'll also know which areas she couldn't see. Our real search will begin there.'

Suddenly, the wind started to push the TARDIS wildly from side to side. Clara began to fall out of the TARDIS, but caught hold of the side of a door at the last second.

'Clara!' shouted the Doctor. 'Come inside! It's dangerous out there.'

Clara wasn't ready to come inside. In fact, she was enjoying her wild,

'With the sonic sunglasses, we can record everything that Clara sees. Then we'll have a map on our computer of what she was looking at.'

windy ride.

'This is great!' she shouted. 'It's more fun than my last birthday party!'

'Enough of that, young lady! You've got a job to do,' the Doctor told her. 'Don't be silly!'

Suddenly, the wind became stronger and the TARDIS turned over again. Clara held tightly to the door, but most of her body was outside the TARDIS.

'I'm flying,' Clara laughed. 'It's wonderful!'

'Clara!' Rigsy shouted. 'Be careful!'

The TARDIS turned again and Clara landed inside.

'It's all good,' Clara told the Doctor and Rigsy. 'Stop worrying. I feel great!'

'You enjoyed that too much!' Rigsy told Clara. 'That was really dangerous!'

'Oh, not really! And I did the job,' Clara said.

After everything calmed down, the three of them looked at the finished map.

'Look!' Clara said. 'There are cloudy areas where my eyes couldn't see things clearly, even with the sonic sunglasses.'

'Those are the areas that we want to look at,' the Doctor said. 'Let's hurry.' He saw the number 217 on Rigsy's neck. Time was passing.

Clara noticed his worried look. Neither of them wanted Rigsy to know how serious the countdown was.

The TARDIS took them to a busy street in the centre of London.

'Clara, you go that way,' the Doctor ordered. 'Local Knowledge, you go the other way. Remember, trap streets are not easy to see. Forget about anything strange or unusual. But if something is boring or uninteresting, take a closer look. And count everything you see: buildings, street signs, traffic lights. When you get close to a trap street, you will probably forget the numbers. That's a sign that one of those streets is near.'

The three searchers chose different areas but stayed close together. Rigsy looked at an ordinary office building. Maybe a little *too* interesting? His search continued. The Doctor pushed through crowds of people. He knew what he was looking for.

As Clara walked along a busy street, she counted everything: her steps, the buildings, windows, shops. Suddenly, she began to smile. What was the last number? She couldn't remember it. She slowed down and started to count again, but again she forgot the numbers. How could that happen?

'This has to be it! I couldn't even count from one to ten,' Clara said to herself. She waved to the Doctor and Rigsy, and shouted, 'Over here. I'm sure there's a trap street near this corner.'

The Doctor and Rigsy joined Clara, and the Doctor said, 'We're very close, but we're thinking about the trap street too much. We have to think about something ordinary, something boring. Then our minds will do the work.

'Clara, go back to the TARDIS. Get me a box full of my most boring things. Bring anything that seems uninteresting. Hurry!'

'Right!' Clara said, and ran away.

She reached the TARDIS quickly, picked up some ordinary things for the Doctor and put them in a plastic box. But as she was leaving the TARDIS, she noticed a light on Rigsy's phone. It was receiving something from the computer. Clara looked and read: INFORMATION FOUND.

She left the plastic box in the TARDIS and ran outside. She needed to talk to the Doctor and Rigsy.

'Clara, where's my box of things?' asked the Doctor, when she reached them again.

'Forget about that,' Clara told him. She showed him the phone. 'Look. Someone called Rigsy's phone yesterday at six o'clock in the morning. The call lasted over a minute, but we don't have the caller's phone number.'

Rigsy reached for his phone. He had a cloudy memory of something from the day before. He dropped the phone as the memory began to form in his mind.

When the phone hit the ground, Rigsy saw – in his mind – the body of a woman on the street. She seemed about forty years old, and wasn't moving. All of this seemed very real to Rigsy, but only he could see it. He looked closely at the woman. She had a very bad cut on the back of her head. Blood was pouring from the cut onto the street.

In his memory, Rigsy wanted to see if the woman was alive. But two aliens suddenly arrived and he was frightened away from the body. The smaller alien was nervous and seemed to be afraid of Rigsy.

But the second alien wasn't afraid. He was big and strong and looked like a wild, hairy animal. He raced to the body, pushed Rigsy away and checked the woman quickly. He said simply, 'She's dead.' Then he and the other alien disappeared as quickly as they came.

'Rigsy, what's wrong?' the Doctor asked. 'You're very quiet. Are you remembering something important?'

Rigsy shook his head as he looked down at the street. What was real and what was a dream? He wasn't sure. But then he looked up and suddenly became even more nervous. He pointed at something behind his two friends. Clara and the Doctor turned to look. But they saw nothing.

'Rigsy, what is it?' Clara asked again. 'There's nothing behind us. What can you see?'

'Look! It's there!' shouted Rigsy. He moved Clara and the Doctor a few steps to the left and pointed again. 'Now can you see it?'

In front of them was the entrance to a dark, narrow street.

'Yes!' Clara answered excitedly. 'I can see it. Doctor, can you see it too?'

'Of course!' the Doctor said. 'This must be the entrance to one of the aliens' streets. But now we have to be even more careful.' He looked at the tattoo on Rigsy's neck. 'There are only fifty minutes left. We have work to do. Local Knowledge, put your hoodie up and pull it low over your face. They know what you look like in there.'

The Doctor guided Clara and Rigsy past the entrance and down the

'Now can you see it?' In front of them was the entrance to a dark, narrow street.

trap street. Then they stopped and looked around. They were in a part of London from the 1500s. There were very old buildings, a rough road, a few horses – but no cars, no electric street lights and, most surprisingly, no people. The three of them were alone.

'Doctor, why did I see the trap street before you and Clara could see it?' asked Rigsy.

'You were thinking about something completely different. A memory escaped from the Retcon and mysteriously appeared in your mind,' the Doctor explained.

Rigsy was worried and didn't want to remember anything about the dead woman. Again and again, he asked himself if that was a real memory. Did he really see a dead body yesterday?

'Where is everybody?' Clara asked. 'Surely other people forget about their plans or lose their way. They must walk down their usual streets without thinking sometimes. Don't they accidentally walk into a trap street?'

'Perhaps they do,' the Doctor agreed. 'It seems possible.'

'Wait! Quiet! What's that?' Clara asked. 'I can hear strange music – and people talking. Are they near us?'

The Doctor took another step along the street. Suddenly, an alarm began to ring and the ground was lit with bright golden lights from some very modern electronic equipment. This didn't look like the 1500s.

'Doctor, what's happening?' Clara asked nervously.

An Old Friend and New Leader

The Doctor, Clara and Rigsy crowded together in a corner of the trap street near the narrow entrance. The alarm was very loud and the golden lights were shining in their eyes.

Suddenly, a tall, strong-looking man hurried into the street. He was about forty years old and looked tired and dangerous. His clothes were old and dirty, like the clothes of a homeless person who lived outside. He moved carefully, watching everything around him. He was clearly a man with secrets, and perhaps a difficult past.

The man pressed one of the stones on the ground with his foot and everything changed. Silence and darkness returned to the street.

After the street returned to its usual look, a little man climbed out of his hiding place below it. He was clearly the big man's companion, but was very different from him. This second man wore glasses and was clean and tidy-looking. But he was also very nervous, and his eyes moved continually from side to side. He watched for anything that moved. He seemed frightened by everything.

The Doctor and his young friends looked at these two men, but again

Rigsy saw things differently. In his eyes only, the two men changed into aliens. The big man became the wild, hairy animal who Rigsy saw earlier next to the woman's body. The small, nervous person became an alien too. But he was more like a little animal with hard, shiny skin. He looked like something that lived under a rock. He seemed afraid and jumped at every sound. Rigsy couldn't believe his eyes. To him, they both looked like animals from a science fiction story, perhaps from a different world. But they were real! They were there – in front of him!

Rigsy saw things differently. In his eyes only, the two men changed into aliens.

Rigsy shook his head and the two men looked like humans again. They were strange-looking, but now they weren't aliens. Rigsy looked at the Doctor and Clara. He couldn't understand. Their faces showed that they didn't see these changes.

The two men, now in human form, turned and saw the Doctor, Clara and Rigsy.

'Three at the same time,' said Kabel, the tidy little man. 'That's new.'

With his nose in the air, the big man, Rump, smelled something unusual. 'Wait a minute,' he said. 'Something isn't right.' He smelled again and came closer to the Doctor. 'This one doesn't smell human.'

Kabel looked closely at the Doctor. 'What's your name?' he asked. 'Where are you from? Why do you need asylum? Hurry. Give us some answers. We haven't got all day.'

'Asylum?' asked the Doctor.

'Yes. The reason you're here. Explain yourself,' said Kabel. 'Why do you need asylum? Where are your papers?'

Rigsy pulled Clara away from the others to talk to her privately. Kabel and Rump were looking at the Doctor and didn't notice them.

Rigsy said quietly to Clara, 'They're not human. They're aliens. I saw them when my mind opened again.'

Kabel was still talking. 'Why didn't they follow the rules?' he asked Rump. 'They haven't even filled in forms.'

Rump looked closely at the Doctor. 'Don't you know that this is a place of asylum?'

'Of course we do,' the Doctor began fearlessly.

'Of course he does!'

A young woman was walking towards them. A group of guards followed her.

Everyone turned to look.

'Of course they know that we offer asylum. You just told them,' said the young woman.

She gave Rump and Kabel a cold look. They began to shake and stayed silent. They were noticeably afraid of her.

Clara was surprised to see an old friend. 'Ashildr?!' she cried.

Hundreds of years before, she and the Doctor helped Ashildr in a difficult fight for her village against aliens.

Ashildr also looked surprised, but quietly pleased. She seemed very young, but was clearly the leader around there. Rump and Kabel watched her carefully, ready to follow her orders.

Ashildr seemed happy to see Clara, but perhaps less comfortable with the Doctor. She nervously touched a piece of cloth which covered her neck.

'Good evening, Madam Mayor,' said Rump and Kabel with fear in their voices.

'Calm down,' Ashildr told them. 'I know these people.'

She turned to Clara and asked, 'Why did you call me Ashildr?'

'Ashildr. It's your name,' the Doctor told her. 'I've told you that a hundred times.'

'Have you?' Ashildr asked. She smiled at Clara. 'Do you know that I will never die? Immortal. That's me! My life never ends. So many people, so many adventures. It's difficult for me to talk to old friends. But I know that you're Clara Oswald. You're as beautiful as your photographs.'

'But we met. Don't you remember? We're friends.' Clara looked sad.

'Of course!' Ashildr said. 'Everything about my past is in my diaries. I have piles of them. I've read our conversations many times. I always enjoy reading them again.'

'That's strange – but sweet,' Clara replied.

'I've been alive for more than one thousand years, so I can't remember everything,' explained Ashildr. 'My diaries help me.'

'Do you remember that you died? Then I helped you come back to life again?' the Doctor asked.

'Yes, and now I can never die. I continue, year after year,' said Ashildr. 'It's not always fun.'

'I've been alive for more than one thousand years, so I can't remember everything,' explained Ashildr.

'Well, you have a strong heart – and a *good* heart,' the Doctor said. 'You give asylum to all sorts of people – and to aliens?'

'It's peaceful here because everyone follows the rules,' explained Ashildr. 'It doesn't matter where people came from. We don't judge people because of their past.'

'But how did *you* get here?' Clara asked. 'The Doctor didn't know where you were for a long time. He has a room full of information about you, but nothing after the early 1800s. I thought you were ... dead?'

Ashildr looked at the Doctor. 'That's not funny,' she said. Then she looked at Clara. 'You know, he's always watching me. He always knows where I am.'

'It's professional interest,' the Doctor said. 'Are you still keeping the world safe from me?'

'The world's still here, isn't it?' Ashildr answered proudly.

'Have you two worked together many times in the past?' Clara asked. She didn't know much about the history between these two since her meeting with Ashildr.

'No, but I made sure that he followed my life through the years. I placed myself in a photograph of you and your students last year. He noticed me in that.'

'Of course I did,' said the Doctor. 'I always notice you. But now we urgently need your help. Someone here has put a Chronolock on our friend. Do you have a Quantum Shade?' The Doctor looked very serious now.

'Good Doctor, you already know that I have one,' Ashildr said with a smile.

'Will you explain Quantum Shades to my friends, or should I? I don't think they understand about them or about Chronolocks,' the Doctor said quietly.

Ashildr turned to the Doctor's companions. 'Quantum Shades are killers. They can kill anyone or anything in any time and space. They use Chronolocks, sometimes in the form of a tattoo. That's their favourite way of putting a Chronolock on someone.

'A Chronolock of that type can look like a number on the criminal's neck. We, of course, only use Chronolocks on bad people. When the tattoo reads zero, the criminal will die.'

Rigsy was listening carefully. As he began to understand, he became more frightened. Was the tattoo really counting down to his death? Was he really a criminal? How did any of this happen to him?

'A Quantum Shade on this street takes the form of a raven. The raven will do the job,' Ashildr continued. 'It works – people around here follow our laws. If they don't, I can call on my Quantum Shade for help. We have a very clear contract. The raven solves my problems – and the problems of this street – very quickly.'

The Doctor pulled Rigsy in front of him. Rigsy pushed his hood away from his face. He turned and showed the tattoo on his neck to Ashildr.

'You did this, didn't you?' the Doctor asked Ashildr.

Ashildr's smile disappeared. Kabel and Rump looked at her and seemed nervous again. She clearly wasn't easy to work for. Or she wasn't when she was unhappy. They both stepped back. Everyone looked fearful, and Ashildr looked angry.

Rump could see Rigsy's face now. 'Ha! I thought I knew that smell from somewhere.' He pointed at Rigsy. 'It's him! He's the murderer.'

'Ashildr, what's happening?' asked Clara.

In answer to Clara's question, Ashildr pulled the cloth from her neck. Now everyone could see an unusual black tattoo which moved slowly and mysteriously around her neck. Only the Doctor and Ashildr understood the meaning of this strange tattoo.

'What have you done to my friend?' the Doctor asked.

'You?! Why did you put the tattoo on Rigsy?' Clara cried. 'He's not a criminal. He's never hurt anybody.'

Rigsy was fearfully watching everyone. Questions crowded into his head. *Am I really going to die when the tattoo reads zero?* he thought. *Why doesn't the Doctor do something?*

'This man is a criminal. He murdered a woman,' Ashildr told them. 'Yes, I ordered the Chronolock for him. He will die when the tattoo reaches zero. The Quantum Shade will make sure of that.'

'You ordered his death?' Clara asked. She couldn't believe her ears. 'Can't you see that he's not guilty?'

'I also gave him enough time to return home to his family – to say goodbye. I was kind,' Ashildr said.

'You Retconned him!' shouted the Doctor. 'You took away his memory of yesterday. He had no idea that he had to say goodbye to anyone.'

'We Retcon *all* of our unwanted visitors. We will Retcon you too. Neither of you will remember your visit to us,' Ashildr told them.

'You're not going to Retcon *me!*' shouted Clara.

'Wait! Ashildr, why don't you tell us about yesterday? When you Retcon us, we'll forget this conversation. We can't hurt you with a lost memory. Why did you order Rigsy's death?' the Doctor asked. 'You can tell us everything about it now. We'll forget your reasons when you Retcon us.'

'OK, I'll tell you. Mr Kabel, Mr Rump, bring our guests inside,' Ashildr ordered.

'No!' shouted the Doctor. 'Clara, Rigsy, stop! Ashildr, first I need a promise from you.'

'Now what?' asked Ashildr.

'One of my friends, this young man, is in danger because of you. Promise that the other one will be safe. Promise that you will protect Clara,' the Doctor said.

'Doctor, please. Don't worry about me. I can protect myself,' Clara said fearlessly.

'I promise that Clara Oswald will be safe. That is my personal promise. Nobody will hurt her in any way.' Ashildr turned to Kabel and Rump. 'Do you understand?' she asked them.

'We will follow your orders, Madam Mayor,' Kabel replied.

'Come this way,' Ashildr told the Doctor, Clara and Rigsy.

They all walked farther along the aliens' trap street. Rump and Kabel followed behind them with Ashildr's guards.

Rump came closer to Rigsy and spoke quietly. 'Murderer!' he said.

Clara turned to face Rump. 'What did you say?'

To Rigsy, Rump and Kabel looked like aliens again for a second. Then they changed back into human form.

Rigsy pointed at Rump. 'He called me a murderer,' he said sadly. 'Again.'

The Most Dangerous Street in London

Clara and Rigsy continued to follow Ashildr and the Doctor along the trap street. The guards walked behind them, watching Rigsy carefully.

'What kind of place is this, Clara?' Rigsy asked. 'Have you ever seen anywhere like it in all your travels with the Doctor?'

'No, it's new to me too,' Clara agreed. 'It's full of surprises – it's unbelievable. They've mixed together buildings and vehicles and other equipment from the last six hundred years. A lot of things look old and broken, but others look modern and useful. Look at that. Is it the body of a spaceship?'

'Have you noticed the street lights? How do they work?' Rigsy added. 'What's inside them? Are those worms?'

'And there are some strange plants in those window boxes. But look through that window on your right. There's an ordinary family eating their supper,' Clara said. 'It's a mysterious place.'

'Look higher. Above the street,' Rigsy told Clara. 'Is that a raven in that old cage?'

The black bird in the cage made a frightening sound when it saw the two young people. Its eyes never left Rigsy as he walked along the street.

'I think it *is* a raven,' Clara agreed. 'It's the right size, and it's very black.'

'Clara, is it the Quantum Shade? It's watching my neck. Is it waiting to kill me? Can we go away from it now?' Rigsy looked nervously up at the raven. 'I don't want to see its eyes.'

They continued down the street and noticed strange people. They looked human and were busy with everyday activities, but there was something unusual and not completely human about each of them. Also, it was clear that they knew something about Rigsy. When they saw him, they became watchful or angry. A man picked up a piece of wood for protection. An old woman covered her grandson's eyes. Clearly, she didn't want Rigsy to frighten the child.

Poor Rigsy looked sad, and also frightened. Everyone here believed Rump's story. To them, Rigsy was a murderer. There was no question about that.

'Clara, wait. Look,' he said. 'There really are some unusual people around here. Look at that boy in the doorway on your left.'

He pointed to a boy of about fourteen. The child's eyes were red from crying, but he looked straight at Clara. Then he turned quickly and disappeared into a house.

'Did you see that, Clara?' asked Rigsy excitedly. 'He had a second face on the back of his head. Have you ever seen anyone with two faces?'

In front of Rigsy and Clara, the Doctor and Ashildr continued their conversation.

'So you're calling yourself "Madam Mayor" now?' asked the Doctor.

'Yes, why not? I make the rules in this street, so "Mayor" is my title. It makes me more like you. "Mayor" for me is similar to "Doctor" for you. We have to be as important and wise as our titles, don't we?' Ashildr asked him.

'It's difficult, isn't it?' the Doctor answered. 'Can anyone be wise all the time? In every place? But how long have you been here?'

'I'm sure that you already know the answer to that question. It's in my diaries, but probably about two hundred years. Really, Doctor, why is that important?

'Listen to me, Doctor,' Ashildr continued. '*This* is what's important. You must be very careful. Some of your greatest enemies are very close to you here. This is the most dangerous street in London. But don't worry. I'm the boss here, and I keep this place peaceful and safe.'

Clara and Rigsy joined the Doctor and Ashildr.

'That's an interesting conversation,' said Clara. 'But now can we talk about Rigsy and the Chronolock? He's the person in *real* danger around here. Why do you want him dead?'

'It's better if we go inside first. This crowd doesn't like murderers,' Ashildr said.

'You're right,' the Doctor agreed. 'But tell me: how can everyone here look human? How is that possible?'

'It's not a mystery. It's the Lurkworms,' Ashildr explained. She pointed at one of the fat bright worms inside a street light. 'The light from the Lurkworms makes everything look ordinary to the viewer. Each person sees his or her own real world in the Lurkworms' light.'

It was true. In the light from the Lurkworms, the Doctor saw more than an ordinary human could see. In fact, he could see the two looks that each person had: a human face and body, and a true alien face and body. He was lucky. He could switch between each person's two looks. He quickly noticed that the 'people' around him were really from different alien worlds. He also knew that some of these aliens were very dangerous.

Ashildr saw the Doctor's face when he realised this.

'Don't worry,' she told him. 'I do my job very well. As I told you, you're perfectly safe on my street.'

'You can say that. But to my knowledge, it's not always true. The words "You're perfectly safe" are usually followed by fighting. Then there's a lot of screaming and blood and death,' the Doctor said.

'Not here. Everyone has agreed to my rules. No fighting. If you hurt someone, you must leave the street immediately,' Ashildr explained. 'Or die.'

As they walked along the street, people shouted at Rigsy: 'Go home!' 'We don't want people like you around here!' 'Murderer!'

Ashildr led the Doctor, Clara and Rigsy into a building which was the hospital for the trap street. Guards stood at the door.

Was this the woman from Rigsy's memory?

'There has been no fighting on this street for a hundred years.' Ashildr continued. 'Everything was calm and peaceful until your friend attacked one of our local women. She was weak, but very popular.'

'Wait a minute!' cried Clara. 'How did Rigsy get here? How did he find the entrance to this street? It wasn't easy for us to find it. And we were looking. You need to explain that to us.'

She stopped talking when she saw an unusual box in the middle of the room. It looked like a cage made of bright green light. Inside this cage, they could see a dead woman. Her eyes were closed, and they could see a lot of blood on the back of her head. Was this the woman from Rigsy's memory?

The Doctor looked closely at the cage as Ashildr talked about the woman's death.

'Rump and Kabel found her near the entrance to the street. Somebody probably knocked her down, but we don't know why. Then she probably died from the cut on her head.'

'Probably?!' shouted Clara. 'You put that tattoo, that Chronolock thing, on Rigsy, but you're not even sure about the facts. Really? Is that how you judge a person?'

'My people found him next to the body. Everyone was angry and frightened. I had to act quickly. I needed to protect the street,' Ashildr explained.

'This is crazy! You can't judge Rigsy without more information!' cried Clara. 'He did *not* kill this woman. I *know* that he's not guilty.'

'What was her name?' Rigsy asked. He felt ill. In his mind, he could see the dead woman on the street. He was standing next to her and wanted to help her.

'Anah. Her name was Anah. We're keeping her here until her family comes for the body,' Ashildr told Rigsy. But she clearly wasn't thinking about Anah or Rigsy, and she wasn't listening to Clara. She was watching the Doctor. 'Is something wrong, Doctor? You look very serious.'

'She has a second face on the back of her head,' said the Doctor. 'It is covered by blood from her cut. She's a Janus.'

'Yes, she is,' Ashildr agreed. 'She escaped from a terrible place in another world. The people there hated the Janus because they were different. Anah and her child came here looking for asylum.'

'A child?' the Doctor asked excitedly. 'Is her child a daughter?'

'No, a boy,' answered Ashildr. 'His name is Anahson.'

The Doctor looked unhappy at that answer.

'Is that bad?' Clara asked him.

'Not bad, but not helpful. All Janus have two faces. But Janus *females* have one face that can see into the future. And their second face can look back at the past. It's possible for a daughter to see her mother's past. Perhaps even to name her murderer,' the Doctor explained. 'But sadly, this woman didn't have a daughter.'

'I think her son was outside,' said Clara.

'Wait!' Rigsy cried. 'Is it possible that I *am* the murderer? I didn't *plan* to kill anyone, so perhaps it was an accident. Maybe she frightened me, and I acted without thinking.'

'No, Rigsy. An unknown person called you. We know that. The phone call brought you here,' said the Doctor. 'You didn't arrive here accidentally.'

'Rigsy, there is no way that you did this,' Clara said.

'Someone phoned him because they wanted him here?' Ashildr asked. 'Somebody put him next to the dead body?'

She didn't seem to have any knowledge about the early-morning phone call to Rigsy.

'Yes, of course!' shouted Clara. 'And that means that one of your pets, one of your protected aliens, is the real killer.'

Suddenly, there was loud knocking at the hospital door.

'I need to talk to Madam Mayor!' a man shouted loudly.

'Excuse me,' Ashildr said. 'I have to go outside.'

'Yes, please go,' said the Doctor angrily. 'There's nothing to worry about in here. Nothing except a tattoo that now says 41. We have forty-one minutes. It's 7.05 now. By 7.47 Rigsy will be dead.'

Judgment Day for Chronolock Man

The Doctor, Clara and Rigsy were very worried, but they followed Ashildr into the street. There they joined a large crowd. Everyone was watching a sixty-year-old man who, like Rigsy, had a Chronolock tattoo on his neck.

'Please, Madam Mayor,' Chronolock Man cried. 'I stole the medicine to save my wife. Lock me up, or throw us out into the real world. But I can't leave her.'

The man's wife looked at her husband with a sad smile. Then she turned to Ashildr. 'Please, Madam,' she said. 'He's a good man, and I will die without him. Don't kill him. Please! Stop the raven. We will always follow your rules.'

'How many minutes are left on his tattoo?' Ashildr asked Rump.

Rump checked the man's neck. 'There are only two minutes left, Madam Mayor.'

Ashildr faced the crowd. 'This man stole medicine from our hospital,' she told them. 'He broke one of our rules. I know he had a good reason. But he stole from all of us, and he must die. This street is safe because we have rules. Nobody is above the law.'

Everyone in the crowd was silent. They clearly loved their leader. They believed every word that she said. It was very simple for them. Madam Mayor's judgment was final, so this man and Rigsy had to die. The first was a thief; the second was a murderer.

'This man wants to live. He wants me to take off his Chronolock,' Ashildr continued. She touched the tattoo on her own neck. Chronolock Man looked hopeful. 'But I won't. His crime is too great. I will keep our street safe.'

Chronolock Man knew that he was almost out of time.

His wife held his arm. 'Please – give it to me,' she said to him. 'Say "yes" and it will move to my neck. One word. Say it. Say "yes".'

'No. I stole the medicines because I wanted to save you. You, my lovely wife, are being silly now. You have the medicine and can live a long life. That was my plan, and it has worked,' said the man. He looked at his wife with love and sadness in his eyes.

'What's happening?' asked Rigsy.

'You remember that Ashildr has a contract with a Quantum Shade?' the Doctor said. 'When it puts a Chronolock on a person, the Shade can follow him or her anywhere in this world or in other worlds. It stays with that person for a lifetime, even for a very short lifetime. When the person's tattoo reaches zero, the Shade moves towards him like smoke. I'm sorry about this. I know that isn't good news for you. But I'm afraid that nobody can escape from a Quantum Shade.'

Clara and Rigsy suddenly had a quick view of Chronolock Man and his wife in their true form. Like Rump and Kabel, they were really aliens. When they changed back into human forms, the number 1 was in plain view on the man's tattoo.

With a loud cry, Ashildr uncovered the tattoo on her neck. It came alive and flew away from her body in the form of black smoke.

Chronolock Man saw the smoke and screamed.

When Ashildr's tattoo moved, the raven – in its cage – changed into black smoke. It left its cage as smoke, but then changed into a black bird again. As a raven, it flew into the sky and landed on a rooftop above Chronolock Man. It watched and waited for the man's tattoo to change one final time. To zero.

The man looked straight into the raven's eyes. Then he pushed his wife away and began to run.

'Don't go!' the man's wife shouted wildly at her husband.

But the man was too frightened to listen to her. He ran into the nearest house and shut the door behind him. The raven immediately flew after him but had to stop. It couldn't kill the man until the tattoo read zero.

'Why do they always run?' Kabel asked Rump. 'They know that won't stop the raven.'

When the raven reached the closed door, it changed into black smoke again. It easily passed through the thick wood and into the house.

The crowd were nervous, but watchful and silent. They were surprised when Chronolock Man came out of another house, further down the street. Again, he began to run.

The Doctor spoke quietly to Ashildr. 'Give him an easy death, without pain. You can do that.'

'We don't punish criminals with an easy death. He broke the law. He has to face the raven,' Ashildr said coldly.

Someone saw Chronolock Man's tattoo as he ran past. 'It's time!' he shouted. 'The tattoo says zero!'

The raven flew straight into Chronolock Man, from behind. The man's head went back immediately and his arms flew up. His body, from head to foot, froze in pain. A terrible scream left his dying body.

People covered their ears. Chronolock Man's wife closed her eyes and fell to the ground. When a stream of black smoke came out of the man's mouth, his body also dropped to the ground. He was dead.

There was silence.

The black smoke returned to Ashildr's neck and formed her tattoo again.

The Search for the Real Murderer

The crowd began to leave the street. The Doctor noticed that Ashildr looked unhappy. She was clearly sad about this death.

Ashildr turned to the Doctor. 'I don't want to hurt your friend. Show me and my people that he's not a murderer. If he's not guilty, I'll take away his Chronolock. I don't enjoy watching the raven at work.'

She left the Doctor, Clara and Rigsy in the street.

'OK,' Clara began. 'We have a job to do. We have to talk to these people. Surely someone here knows something. Doctor, I'll be the kind police officer – the one that people like. You'll be the bad police officer – the one who frightens them. We'll see what we can find out.'

'Wait a minute!' the Doctor shouted. 'Why can't I be the *kind* officer sometimes?'

'Doctor, we've discussed this in the past. Have you looked in a mirror? Nobody can imagine you as a kind police officer.'

'You're right. But let's forget about police. We don't have to find the real killer. We simply have to show these people that Rigsy isn't the murderer. And we have to work fast!'

The Doctor hurried away. He wanted to ask a lot of questions. He had to find out everything about Anah's murder. Somebody knew something about her death.

Rigsy was sitting near the entrance to the hospital, talking to Jen and their daughter on the telephone.

'Lucy, baby girl, please stop crying.'

Jen said, 'She's been like this all day. She misses you.'

'Lucy, listen. Be good for your mum, OK? I miss you both – and I'm trying to get home to you,' Rigsy said very softly.

'She can't stop crying,' Jen told Rigsy. 'She senses that something's wrong.'

'I know. I can hear her. She knows that you're worried,' Rigsy said. 'Try to stay calm if you can, Jen.'

Clara was watching. She could see how difficult this was for Rigsy. Her heart was breaking for him. She had to help him, and she had an idea.

She saw Rump and hurried across the street to him.

'Rump? Your name's Rump, isn't it?' Clara began. 'I heard the dead man's wife talking to him. It seemed important. She said, "Give it to me. Say 'yes' and it will move to my neck." What did she mean? Was she talking about the tattoo on her husband's neck?'

'Yes, of course. There are two ways to stop a death from a Quantum Shade,' Rump explained. 'Everyone here knows that. Madam Mayor can take the Chronolock off – or the person with the tattoo can give it to another person.'

'Give it? Just give it to anyone?' Clara asked.

'No, it's not that simple. It's not a game,' Rump told her. 'The other person has to request the tattoo and has to understand the result. They can't escape death. You can pass the tattoo to another person, but you can't change the Quantum Shade's contract. If the Shade has agreed to kill someone for Ashildr, that's the contract. Someone has to die.'

Out of the corner of her eye, Clara saw the Janus boy, Anahson. He was standing in the shadows, looking at her. But when Clara waved, the boy hurried away.

Clara quickly forgot about Anahson. She had to think about her conversation with Rump. Could this new information help Rigsy in some way? She hurried to him.

Rigsy listened to Clara, but couldn't believe her.

'Clara, really? You can't be serious!' Rigsy said. 'You want me to give you my death tattoo? You want to die for me?'

'Well,' Clara said playfully, 'I've always wanted a tattoo. Something small and pretty. Something sensible. Are tattoos ever sensible?'

'Clara!' Rigsy said. 'Stop joking!'

'Weren't you listening?' Clara asked. 'Madam Mayor promised to protect me. That's a law now, I think. The raven is working for her, so it can't hurt me. Don't you think this is a very clever plan?'

'No, no! It's a dangerous plan – for both of us!' shouted Rigsy. 'I refuse to put you in danger.'

'Listen! Madam Mayor has to follow her own rules.' Clara stopped and thought for a minute. 'I'm beginning to think like the Doctor!' she said proudly. 'When the tattoo reaches zero, in about thirty minutes, everybody will see it on my neck. Ashildr will stop the raven killing me because she promised to protect me. And we'll have more time to find the real killer.'

'The Doctor won't like this,' Rigsy told her. 'He'll agree with me. It's a crazy plan.'

'But I've learned many lessons from the Doctor. One of them is: Keep your plans secret,' Clara explained. 'He'll be really angry, and he'll shout at Ashildr. She'll probably take the Chronolock off to stop the shouting.' She could see that Rigsy was still very worried by her plan. 'Rigsy, what's going to happen to your family if you die?' she asked. 'Do you really want your little daughter to grow up without a father? You must be brave for Lucy and Jen. You must try everything for them.' Rigsy looked even more worried. 'Rigsy, believe me. My plan gives us hope.' Clara was thinking and talking like the Doctor. 'We can do this. Don't be afraid.'

Finally, Rigsy agreed. 'OK, Clara. How do we do it?'

'Perhaps it's easy. I say that I want it. I've done that. You say that I can have it. You've done that,' Clara said. 'Now show me the tattoo.'

Rigsy pulled his hood down. When Clara touched the tattoo, he felt a sharp pain. Suddenly, the tattoo changed into black smoke and left Rigsy's neck. The smoke moved into Clara's mouth. Then Clara also felt a sharp pain when the tattoo hit the skin on the back of her neck.

The business was done. Clara pulled her jacket up to cover the tattoo. It now showed thirty-three minutes.

Above the street, the raven felt alarmed and cried out. Something was different. There was a new name on the contract.

The Doctor was busy asking questions about Anah's murder.

'Are you sure that the murderer wasn't somebody from the street? Isn't that possible?' he asked Rump.

'I told you already,' said Rump. 'There were only two people at that end of the street: Anah and the human.'

'But there are about twenty-seven types of aliens on this street. More than half of that number get angry very easily. They fight with everybody. Aren't there some groups on the street that have enemies? Isn't it possible that one of them hated Anah? And maybe wanted her dead?'

'A lot of them have murdered somebody. But none of them wanted to kill Anah,' Rump said.

'Why not? Why was she special?' the Doctor asked.

Two women heard the Doctor's question. One of them said, 'It was the way that she looked at you. She seemed to understand your problems.'

'She could see into your past. She felt your pain,' the second woman added. 'Everybody will miss Anah.'

The Doctor felt angry now. 'You want the human dead. Isn't that right? You can't prove that Rigsy is the killer.'

'Don't you understand?' Rump said. 'The murderer has to be him or one of us. If it's one of us … No, I can't even think about it. We can't fight our neighbours. The street has to be a safe place. We all need asylum here.'

'So Rigsy will die?' asked the Doctor. 'Even if he's not guilty?'

'Yes, he must, to keep our world safe and peaceful,' replied Rump.

He didn't seem proud of the idea – of killing Rigsy. But he clearly couldn't see a better way to protect the street.

When Clara left Rigsy, she tried to talk to a small group of people on the next corner. They moved away from her as quickly as possible. They weren't interested in talking to a stranger about Rigsy or about Anah's death.

Clara knew that the number on her neck was very low. She saw the Doctor farther down the street, talking to Kabel. She held up ten fingers and then two. Twelve minutes left!

The Doctor's face showed that he understood.

'Why are you so sure that Rigsy's the murderer?' the Doctor asked Kabel.

'He seemed afraid of us. He called for a doctor when he saw me and Rump,' Kabel explained.

'*What? What* did he do?' the Doctor asked excitedly. 'He was afraid? And *then* what?'

'He asked Madam Mayor to call a doctor. Poor Anah was already dead. Dead – there at his feet,' Kabel told the Doctor. 'The human was only worried about himself.'

'Be quiet! Listen to me very carefully,' the Doctor ordered. 'Did Rigsy say "*a* doctor" or "*the* doctor"? This is very, very important. Try to remember.'

Kabel thought very hard. '*The* doctor. But there wasn't anything wrong with him. He wasn't sick – or hurt. It was the usual human lies.'

The Doctor turned and ran down the street. He found Clara and Rigsy and pulled them into a doorway. He spoke quietly to Rigsy.

'Clara gave you my phone number. You could use it if you were in danger. If you had a serious problem. So this morning you woke up with a strange tattoo on your neck and no memory of the past twenty-four hours. What did you do?'

'I called *you*,' Rigsy answered.

'Yes! Now think about the dead woman. You were on an unknown street in the middle of central London. The people there took your phone. They pointed at you and called you a murderer. So you asked the boss – Ashildr – to call "the Doctor". You wanted her to call me. She's known me for hundreds of years. Why didn't she tell you that at that time? And why did she hide your request from me?' The Doctor was trying to put the pieces of the last twenty-four hours together. 'Why didn't she call me immediately? She didn't because it didn't fit into her plan.'

'Doctor, there are only twelve minutes left. We need to think fast,' Clara told him.

'But Clara,' Rigsy began, 'if there *is* a murderer here, nobody will tell us. The way they look at me …'

'The way they look at you?' Clara repeated. She had an idea.

'*What? What* did he do?' the Doctor asked excitedly. 'He was afraid? And *then* what?'

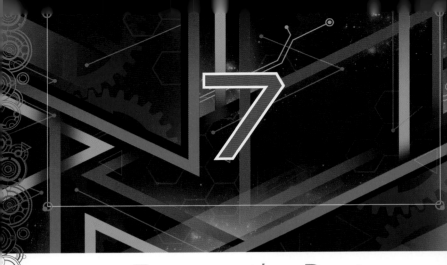

Eyes on the Past

Clara turned and walked towards a house not far away. Rigsy and the Doctor followed her. Clara was sure that the house belonged to Anah and her son. She knocked and Anahson nervously opened the door. He didn't look at Clara. He looked straight into the Doctor's eyes.

'Hi, Anahson,' Clara began in a friendly voice. She wanted him to look at her. 'None of the people around here want to talk to us. They don't want to be near us, but you seem different. I think you want to know more about us. Is that true?'

'I don't know what you mean,' Anahson said shyly. His eyes showed that he was frightened.

'I'm sure you do. You know that Rigsy didn't kill your mother. You can see the past, can't you? You know that it wasn't him.' Clara was sure that she was right. She could see it in Anahson's eyes.

'Your mother dressed you as a boy, didn't she?' Clara continued. 'She wanted to protect you. But you're a girl, aren't you? You can see the future – and the past. You have the gift.'

'It isn't a gift! It only brings trouble. I'm safe here – as a boy. I can't throw that away,' Anahson cried. 'This is the first place in my life where I've felt safe.'

'What is the mayor doing? What is she planning?' the Doctor asked. 'It's nothing good, is it?'

'I can't see everything,' Anahson tried to explain. 'But she thinks that she's doing the right thing.'

'Strong leaders like her usually do believe that they have all the answers,' the Doctor said. 'Can you tell us if her plans are dangerous or not? If not, we'll keep your secret. But if she's planning something bad ...'

'I don't know her plans exactly,' Anahson told them. 'I can't see that part of the future.'

'Why not?' the Doctor asked.

'Because there's something about *you* in her plans. When I look at you, your past and future are mixed together. And there is so much of both. I don't understand.' As Anahson said this, her front eyes closed. The eyes at the back of her head opened. She tried very hard to see into the Doctor's past.

'This isn't about Rigsy,' the Doctor said sadly. 'It's about me.'

'I'm afraid that's true,' Anahson said. 'Madam Mayor couldn't just invite you here, like an old friend. She needed a mystery, something that was interesting and important for you. She thought of a story about my mother and Rigsy. Rigsy was in terrible trouble. Of course you came here to help him. Madam Mayor was not surprised, because you always try to help your friends. It was her plan.' She thought for a minute. 'Wait! I can see something more. She's afraid.'

'Afraid of what?' asked the Doctor urgently. 'Of who?'

'I can't see,' Anahson said. 'I'm sorry. Really sorry.'

The Doctor, Clara, Rigsy and Anahson raced down the street. As they passed the cage above their heads, the raven made a terrible, frightening noise. It sounded like a scream from a different world.

'You! Be quiet! We have ten more minutes. Give us time to do our work,' the Doctor shouted at the black bird.

They hurried to the hospital and looked at Anah in her cage.

Why is she still here? the Doctor asked himself. 'Think about this,' he told the others. 'The Janus burn their dead. Is there a reason for the cage and for keeping Anah in it?'

'Doctor, we have to hurry!' Rigsy said.

But the Doctor was thinking. 'There's a mystery here, and I need to solve it.'

He looked at the cage carefully. He touched the green light, and suddenly a small computer lit up.

'Doctor, what do you see?' Anahson asked.

'It's information about your mother's health,' the Doctor said.

'But she's dead. Why is that important now?' Anahson asked sadly.

The Doctor touched the computer and saw something new. 'I'm not sure that Anah is dead. Look at this. This light is moving exactly like a living heart. The cage and its equipment are keeping Anah alive. This computer is recording information about her body. Her *living* body.'

'She's alive?' Anahson cried.

'Yes, she's alive,' the Doctor told her.

'Get her out of there! Please!' shouted Anahson.

The Doctor tried everything, but he couldn't free Anah.

'There has to be a way to unlock the cage,' he said.

'A keyhole!' shouted Rigsy.

'Yes, thank you, very helpful,' the Doctor replied. 'Why didn't *I* think of a keyhole?'

'Doctor, look!' Rigsy shouted again. 'There *is* a keyhole at the side of the cage.'

'You're right! But where's the key?' the Doctor said.

'I'll find Madam Mayor,' Anahson said. 'I'll ask her for the key. Maybe there was no murder.'

'Yes, tell her … ' the Doctor began. 'No, wait. It's part of her plan. Your great leader wants us to free your mother. But she's disappeared because she doesn't want us to use *her* key. She wants me to use *mine*.'

He took the TARDIS key out of his pocket.

'The TARDIS key? Is that what she wants?' asked Clara.

The Doctor put the key to the TARDIS into the keyhole. It turned smoothly.

The information on the computer went crazy. Everyone looked at Anah.

The Doctor turned the key again and a heavy metal bracelet closed around his wrist.

'Doctor! Wait!' Clara cried. 'Pull the key out!'

'No, Clara,' said the Doctor. 'Anahson needs her mother.'

He turned the key the opposite way and pulled his arm away from the

'The Janus burn their dead. Is there a reason for the cage and for keeping Anah in it?'

cage. The strange metal bracelet was still on his wrist.

'What is that thing?' asked Clara.

'And where's the key?' added Rigsy.

They looked at the cage again. Both the keyhole and the key were gone.

Suddenly, Anah began to move.

'Mum!' cried Anahson.

Anah was very weak, but she was able to leave the cage. Clara and Rigsy guided her into her daughter's arms. The two of them sat on the floor, and Anah began to wake up. The cut on her head closed, and her skin looked perfect again.

'Mum, are you really OK?' Anahson asked.

'She'll be perfectly fine in a few minutes, I promise you.' Everybody was surprised to hear Ashildr's voice. She was standing at the door, watching them.

'There are easier ways to steal a key,' the Doctor told Madam Mayor.

A Brave New Prisoner

'I don't want your TARDIS,' Ashildr told the Doctor. 'This isn't about your silly flying time machine.' She looked around for Rigsy. 'Come here, Rigsy,' she ordered. 'I'll take off the Chronolock. You've been useful, but your death isn't important now.'

Rigsy looked at Clara for help, but she was watching the Doctor. He was using his sonic sunglasses on the heavy bracelet without success. He couldn't understand why the sonic sunglasses couldn't help him this time. After a few tries, he gave up and returned the sunglasses to their usual pocket.

'What is this bracelet?' the Doctor asked Ashildr. 'It won't keep me here.'

'Don't you know?' Ashildr answered in her sweetest voice. 'It's a teleport bracelet.'

'What?' asked Clara.

Ashildr continued to speak to the Doctor. 'I'll give you time to say goodbye. Don't worry, you're safe. Nobody will hurt you. But with the teleport, the Quantum Shade will be able to move you anywhere in the world. Or to another world. You see, you don't need the TARDIS now.'

'So, where am I going?' the Doctor asked Ashildr.

'That's not my business. I made an agreement: First, I get you here. After that, they take you and I take the key. Then nobody can find you. They make the rules, and I follow them. The street and its people stay safe.'

'*They?* Who are *they?*' the Doctor asked.

'You know who they are. Don't worry about that. But there's one more thing that they want. You have to give me your Confession Dial,' Ashildr told him.

She put out her hand and waited. 'They'll take it from you if they have to. But I think you have it in one of your pockets. Am I right? Just give it to me. You've already lost.'

The Doctor pulled a Confession Dial from his pocket and Ashildr took it. She looked at it carefully.

'What is this thing?' she asked. 'I've never seen one before. How does it work?'

'This little disk is very important to me, but I don't understand *your* need for it,' the Doctor said. 'It holds my final thoughts and requests. Every Gallifreyan carries one of these. We Gallifreyans give our Confession Dials to our closest friend on the night before our death. I'm afraid that you're robbing me of that adventure. How does it work, you ask? I have no idea.'

'Well, thank you,' Ashildr said. 'Now, Rigsy, your neck.'

'Clara, tell them. The Chronolock ...,' said Rigsy.

'What do you mean?' asked Ashildr.

'I'll tell you after you take the teleport off the Doctor's wrist,' Clara told Ashildr.

Ashildr looked at Rigsy's neck. She began to understand.

'Listen! I don't have the Chronolock. Clara does!' shouted Rigsy.

'No, this can't be possible,' Ashildr cried.

Clara showed her neck to Ashildr and to the Doctor. Everyone could see that there were only two minutes left.

'Quickly,' she said. 'Take the teleport off.'

'Clara, you didn't!' cried the Doctor. He was as white as a sheet.

'How could she be so stupid?' Ashildr asked. 'How could this happen? This was *not* part of my plan. I didn't mean to hurt anyone.' She looked at Clara. 'What were you *thinking?* How can *your* death help Rigsy?'

'I didn't plan to die,' Clara said quietly. 'I was safe. Didn't you say that?

I wanted more time to find the real murderer. And now – aren't you going to protect me?'

'Rigsy!' shouted the Doctor. 'Why did you do this?'

'It wasn't *him*. It was *my* idea. Just *mine!*' Clara shouted. 'I talked to Rump, and he said …'

'What exactly did Rump say?' the Doctor asked.

'The Shade has a contract for a death. But you can pass the Chronolock to another person, and then …' Clara stopped suddenly. She was beginning to understand the problem. The great big problem. 'But …' Her voice was shaking. There was real fear in her eyes now.

'But *what?*' asked the Doctor urgently.

'But she is going to die,' Ashildr explained sadly. 'Look at the tattoo. Nobody can stop it. Nobody can protect Clara from it – not even me.'

'Clara,' Rigsy said, 'you didn't tell me everything. Give the tattoo back to me. Now! Nobody wanted to kill you.'

'She *can't* give it back to you,' Ashildr said. 'Yes, Clara, I made a contract with the Quantum Shade when I put the Chronolock on Rigsy. I promised it a life, and only I could break that contract. But when you took the Chronolock from Rigsy, you changed the contract.

'Look at my tattoo,' Ashildr continued, pointing at her neck. 'It's not moving because you cut me out of the contract. Now it's between you and the Quantum Shade. I can do nothing for you.'

It was very dark now, but the raven was awake. It was getting excited, and ready for its next job. It was almost time to act. It turned into black smoke and flew out of its cage. Then it became a bird again and flew along the street.

Clara looked at the Doctor. There was still hope in her eyes.

'But Doctor, we can make this right – can't we? We *always* solve problems, don't we?' Her voice was becoming shakier.

'Not this time, Clara. I can't make this right – but *you* can,' the Doctor said, pointing at Ashildr. 'Do something. Now!'

'I'm very, very sorry, but it's not possible. I can't,' Ashildr said unhappily. 'I planned to save Rigsy, but I can't save you, Clara.'

The Doctor's face turned red and he began to shout very loudly. 'It *has* to be possible! You *can* and you *will* make this right. If you don't, I will destroy you and all your funny little friends. I have alien friends too. I think you know some of them. I'll bring the Zygons, the Daleks and the Cybermen*. They will be happy to destroy this street. You *will* save Clara or I will destroy *you* again and again.'

'Doctor, stop talking like that!' Clara cried.

'You can't do that to me,' Ashildr said nervously.

'I can, and I will!' the Doctor shouted at her. 'You've read the stories about me. You know who I am. You know what I can do. In all your long history, was there anyone who could stop me?'

Silence seemed to fill the room.

Ashildr looked more and more frightened. Finally, she said, 'I know you. You won't hurt me. You aren't that kind of Doctor. You're a *good* Doctor.'

'That Doctor is gone. And I will destroy you, and everything that you love,' the Doctor said. He looked into Ashildr's eyes with real hate.

'Doctor, please. Please, will you stop?' Clara cried.

'No! Never!' the Doctor shouted.

'*I* did this, do you hear me? It's *my* problem,' said Clara.

'I know,' the Doctor replied, more quietly. 'But it's also *my* problem now. I'm not going to worry about anyone or anything.'

'You're lying. You *always* worry. You always have. You're soft and kind and good. You help everyone – every hungry person, every crying baby, every dying soldier. You'll stop fighting now because you worry about every one of them.'

'No, I don't,' answered the Doctor coldly.

'I know you. Now listen to me,' Clara said. 'If these are our final minutes

*the Zygons, the Daleks and the Cybermen: three alien groups. Each group has a different skill which can help the Doctor in a fight against Ashildr.

together … please, don't be so angry.'

The Doctor knew what was coming. His heart was breaking. He was speechless.

Clara looked at Ashildr. 'Is there anything you can do?'

'I'm sorry,' said Ashildr. 'I'm truly sorry.'

'There's very little time,' replied Clara. 'Yes or no?'

'No,' Ashildr said softly. 'I can do nothing.'

'Well, that's that,' Clara said. She stood up straight, as tall as possible. She thought about an old boyfriend who became part of the Doctor's world. As a result he died twice, bravely, like the true soldier that he was. 'But if Danny Pink can do it, I can too.'

'Do what?' the Doctor asked quietly.

'Have a good death. Die bravely. Face the raven without fear,' Clara said in a strong voice.

'No!' shouted the Doctor. 'This is *not* going to happen.'

'Today my luck has ended,' Clara said. 'But who knows? Maybe this is what I wanted. Why did I do all those dangerous things? What did I want to prove?'

'You were helping me,' the Doctor said sadly.

'Yes, because I wanted to. I didn't *have* to travel with you on the TARDIS. I loved our adventures,' Clara said.

'Our adventures – our journeys – became more and more dangerous,' replied the Doctor. 'You weren't safe.'

'I loved everything we did. And your life is dangerous all the time! Why should *you* get all the fun? What's so special about *you*?' laughed Clara.

'Clara, be serious. I'm not special. I'm nothing. But I'm stronger than you. Why didn't I protect you?'

'I never asked you to protect me,' Clara told him.

'But I wanted to. You didn't have to ask. I *wanted* to – but I've failed.'

Face the Raven

The aliens heard the noise of the raven's cry and looked up. They watched the black bird fly down the street.

Everyone around Clara – the Doctor, Rigsy, Anah and Anahson – was worried and sad. Nobody knew how to help her. Was there nothing that anyone could do?

'Clara, why didn't ...?' Rigsy began.

'Rigsy! Be quiet!' Clara shouted.

'But ...' Rigsy tried again.

'Seriously, Rigsy, be quiet. It's my problem, not yours. You must *not* feel bad about this.'

All of them heard the raven outside.

'Oh, it's here,' Clara said, as she looked towards the door. She was terribly frightened, but she wanted to be calm. She tried to empty her mind. She wanted to be quiet and to think about the important things in her life.

She turned to the Doctor and said, 'You! Listen! You're going to be alone now, and you're bad at that. You're going to be really angry and really sad. But listen to me. Don't change anything. You are the Doctor.'

'Clara, please ...' The Doctor tried to speak.

'No, listen. Ashildr, or the Quantum Shade, is going to send you somewhere. Who knows where? But you'll know what to do. You'll succeed anywhere. Don't be a fighter! Be the Doctor!' Clara told him with feeling.

'I'm not a good Doctor. I can't help *you*.'

'Then help yourself. Don't start hating people. I'm not asking for a promise,' Clara explained. 'I'm giving you an order. There will be *no* revenge. Do *not* destroy memories of me in that way. I will die. Very soon. But nobody here or in any other place will suffer because of my death.'

'What should I do?' asked the Doctor.

'You and I will both have to be brave,' Clara told him.

'Clara …'

She took the Doctor's hand. 'Please be quiet. I already know what you're thinking. Don't say anything. No more talking.'

The Doctor's eyes filled with tears.

Then they heard the raven outside again.

'Clara, stay here with me,' the Doctor asked. 'Don't run!'

But Clara didn't want to die there with her friends around her. She wanted them to remember when she was alive and strong. Her eyes were shining. She felt proud and brave.

'No. You stay here, Doctor. In the end, everybody has to face death alone,' she said in a clear voice.

'Clara, please!' the Doctor cried.

'I'm being as brave as I can be. I know that my death will hurt you,' she told the Doctor. 'But can I ask you for one thing? Be a little proud of me.'

She touched the Doctor's face. He looked at his companion with great sadness and quietly kissed her hand.

'Goodbye, Doctor,' Clara said softly.

The Doctor couldn't speak as he watched Clara leave.

Clara's back was towards the Doctor. As she walked out of the door, he couldn't see the frightened look in her eyes.

Clara heard the raven's loud inhuman call. Then she saw it flying towards her. It was time. She walked slowly towards the raven. Tears were streaming down her face. She was terribly afraid, but she repeated one sentence again and again:

'I'm going to be brave.

I'm going to be brave.

I'm going to be brave.'

The Doctor and Rigsy hurried to the door and looked out. They could see Clara's back, but not her frightened face. She was completely alone on the street.

Suddenly, the raven flew down and straight into Clara's chest. She cried out in terrible pain. The sound of her cry travelled down the street. Rump looked up. Even his cold heart was breaking for this clever, brave young woman.

The Doctor and Rigsy watched from the doorway. Clara's body froze from the terrible pain. Then the black smoke flew out of her mouth. As the smoke travelled towards the sky, Clara slowly fell to the ground – dead.

For some time, the Doctor couldn't move. He couldn't believe that Clara was gone. Finally, he seemed to wake up. He looked around and saw Rigsy in a corner with his head in his hands.

'Rigsy, go home,' the Doctor said softly. 'You need to be with Jen and your baby. They'll be sick with worry.'

After he said goodbye to Rigsy, the Doctor walked slowly back into the hospital. He found Ashildr at her computer. She stood up and walked towards him.

As Ashildr came near him, the Doctor held out his arm with the teleport bracelet on it. He knew that he was going on a new journey. But this time, he couldn't say where or when.

Ashildr still looked sad. 'I'm sorry, Doctor,' she said. 'I really am.'

She was terribly afraid, but she repeated one sentence again and again: 'I'm going to be brave.'

'Did you hear what Clara said earlier? "No revenge." Why did she say that?' the Doctor asked.

'She was saving you,' explained Ashildr.

'I don't agree,' the Doctor said. 'I was lost a long time ago. She was saving *you*.'

He looked at Ashildr with hate in his eyes. He didn't want to forgive her. He didn't want to be kind and understanding. In that second, he was the most frightening person in this world, and every other world. Ashildr could feel his hate.

'I'll try to follow Clara's request,' he told Ashildr. 'But you should stay out of my way. Stay far, far away.'

The teleport on the Doctor's wrist suddenly lit up. An empty look in the Doctor's eyes made Ashildr even more frightened. She turned away from the Doctor as the light from the teleport bracelet became stronger and stronger.

The Doctor's body changed into bright light, and he suddenly disappeared. He was gone. Completely gone! But the heavy metal teleport bracelet from his wrist fell noisily to the floor.

The room was dark and quiet now, but Ashildr was still there. She looked unusually nervous. She was unsure about everything. More than anything, she was unsure about the Doctor. Where was he now? Was he part of her future, as he was of her past?

But the street was still the most important thing to Ashildr. Was it protected now, after her contract with the Quantum Shade? Could she continue as leader even after Clara's death and the Doctor's terrible exit? Was she guilty of two terrible crimes? Who was judging her?

She looked inside herself. She decided then that this was not her end. She was strong – and immortal. She had work to do. Nobody could stop her.

Activities

Chapters 1-2

Before you read

1 Look at the Word List at the back of the book. Then answer these questions. Discuss your answers with a friend.

    a Do we often or never see *aliens* in our world?
    b Do you wear a *bracelet* on your arm or on your leg?
    c Are *contracts* usually easy or difficult to break?
    d Is *graffiti* usually for sale or not for sale?
    e Is a *criminal* guilty of something or nothing?
    f Is a *hood* useful in hot or cold weather?
    g Do *mayors* work for a city or for themselves?
    h Do *worms* do important work in the house or in the garden?
    i Is it painful or painless to get a *tattoo*?
    j Are great *leaders* usually boring or exciting?

2 How can you use these words when you talk about war? Put them in sentences.

    alarmed   asylum   leader peaceful   revenge

3 Read In this story and the Introduction, at the beginning of the book, and talk about these:

    a Have you seen any of the *Doctor Who* television programmes? If you have, what did you think of them and of the Doctor?
    b In your opinion, is it a good idea for the Doctor to have a human companion? Do you think this adds anything to the story?
    c Imagine that you are in the TARDIS. Think of a time and place for a journey that you would like to go on with the Doctor.
    d Can you name any other TV programmes or films with aliens in them? Do you enjoy this kind of story? Why (not)?

While you read

4 Write D (the Doctor), C (Clara) or R (Rigsy). Who ...

  a has escaped from marriage to a large plant?
  b gave Rigsy the Doctor's phone number?
  c has a tattoo of a number on his neck?
  d painted graffiti on places outside?
  e calls Rigsy 'Local Knowledge'?
  f has a daughter named Lucy?
  g didn't go to work yesterday?
  h owns a pair of sonic sunglasses?
  i checks Rigsy's phone for information?
  j explains the words *Retconned* and *Chronolock?*

After you read

5 Think about Clara's feelings. Is she happy or worried when she is ...

  a talking to the Doctor about their adventure with aliens?
  b talking to Rigsy on the telephone?
  c meeting Lucy?
  d checking Rigsy's phone?
  e learning about Chronolocks?
  f looking at city streets through the sonic sunglasses?
  g noticing a computer message about Rigsy's phone?
  h hearing strange music on the trap street?

  Explain your answers to a friend:
  'I think she is happy/worried because ...'

6 Imagine that Rigsy calls Jen after he arrives at the trap street. He wants to tell her about his surprising day. Act out the conversation with a friend.

Chapters 3-4

Before you read

7 Think about these questions about the trap street.

  a Why did Rigsy see the trap street before Clara and the Doctor saw it?

b Who lives there?

c Why don't ordinary people notice the trap street?

d What did the Doctor, Clara and Rigsy see and hear at the entrance to the street?

8 What did Rigsy remember when he dropped his phone in Chapter 2? Do you think his memories were real or not?

While you read

9 Are these sentences right (✔) or wrong (✗)?

a Rigsy changes into an alien sometimes.

b The Doctor is looking for a place of asylum.

c To Rump, aliens smell different from humans.

d Ashildr is the most important person in the trap street.

e Ashildr seems happy about her immortality.

f Quantum Shades are calm, kind and peaceful.

g Ashildr has a tattoo on her neck.

h Clara believes that Rigsy is a murderer.

i The raven above the trap street frightens Rigsy.

j Ashildr has been on the trap street for many years.

k The Lurkworms are pets for children on the street.

l Anah's body is in the trap street hospital.

m The Doctor notices that Anah is also a Gallifreyan.

n Ashildr is surprised to hear about the phone call to Rigsy yesterday morning.

After you read

10 Why are these important to the story so far? How does each one help to make this a science fiction story?

a Rump and Kabel

b A place of asylum for aliens

c A piece of cloth on Ashildr's neck

d Ashildr's diaries

e A contract with a Quantum Shade

f The Lurkworms

Chapters 5-6

Before you read

11 What do you know now about each of these? How do you think each of them will be important to the story?

a Rigsy's tattoo
b Ashildr's promise to keep Clara safe
c the raven
d the Janus

While you read

12 Follow Chronolock Man's last minutes in Chapter 5. Put these in the correct order (1-5).

a He screams as he dies. ....
b He runs from the raven, into a house. ....
c He asks Ashildr to save him. ....
d He lies dead on the ground. ....
e He tells his wife to live a long, healthy life. ....

13 Circle the correct information about Chapter 6.

a When Chronolock Man dies, Ashildr feels *angry/sad*.
b When the Doctor and Clara decide to find the real murderer, they feel *afraid/purposeful*.
c While Rigsy is away from home, Jen and Lucy feel *worried/calm*.
d When Clara is talking to Rump, she acts like a *teacher/detective*.
e Anahson *wants/doesn't want* to talk to Clara.
f When Rigsy first hears about Clara's plan, he is strongly *against/for* it.
g When the tattoo moves from Rigsy to Clara, the raven feels *surprised/brave*.
h When the Doctor questions Rump about Anah's murder, he becomes *frightened/angry*.
i When the Doctor questions Kabel, he becomes *excited/bored*.

After you read

14 Why do you think Chronolock Man's story comes in Chapter 5, about halfway through the book? How do the Doctor, Clara, Rigsy and Ashildr feel about his death? How do you, as a reader, feel about his story? Does it prepare you for the following chapters?

15 Find these sentences in Chapter 6 and discuss them with a friend. What is happening? How will each of these parts of the story change what happens next?

    a Her heart was breaking for him.
    b There was a new name on the contract.
    c 'And why did she hide your request from me?'

Chapters 7-9

Before you read

16 At the end of Chapter 6, Clara has an idea when she says, 'The way they look at you?'

    a Who are 'they' and 'you' in this sentence?
    b Who in the story has something to do with 'looking'?
       Who do you think Clara wants to talk to?

While you read

17 Write the name of the person who – possibly – has these thoughts:

    a *I want to live as a boy.* ....
    b *I saw that keyhole before the Doctor did.* ....
    c *Anah is more important than my key.* ....
    d *It's wonderful to see my daughter again.* ....
    e *I never planned to kill Rigsy.* ....
    f *A Confession Dial is full of meaning for Gallifreyans like me.* ....
    g *Why can't she keep her promise to protect me?* ....
    h *If Clara dies, I will go to war.* ....

i *I'm not as brave as I seem. I'm afraid of pain and death.* ....

j *I will miss my clever companion more than anyone can imagine.* ....

k *Maybe one day the Doctor will forgive me.* ....

After you read

18 Work with a friend. Solve these mysteries.

a Why has Anahson always dressed as a boy?

b Why can't Anahson see everything in Ashildr's past and future?

c The Janus burn their dead. Why is Anah's body in a cage?

d Why does the TARDIS key open Anah's cage door?

e Why is the idea of Rigsy's death unimportant to Ashildr?

f What is the purpose of a teleport bracelet?

g What is the purpose of a Confession Dial?

h What does Clara not understand about the way a Chronolock works?

i What is Ashildr's reason for agreeing to put the teleport bracelet on the Doctor?

19 After you finish the story, talk about these people. Why are they sad and angry?

a the Doctor   **c** Ashildr

b Rigsy   **d** Chronolock Man's wife

Writing

20 Clara has some time alone while Rigsy is talking to Jen on the phone (in Chapter 6). Clara urgently wants to help Rigsy. How can she save him from the Chronolock? Write her notes on three different ideas.

21 Imagine that Clara does not take the Chronolock from Rigsy. He understands that he is going to die. Write a goodbye letter from him to Jen and Lucy. What does he want to say about his feelings for them? What does he hope for their future? How does he suggest that they plan their lives after his death?

22 'Face the Raven' has a sad ending. Read Chapter 9 again. Then write a different, happier ending to the story.

23 After her death, Clara's friends meet to remember her. A few people make speeches about her. Write a short speech for one of these people to give: the Doctor, Rigsy or Ashildr.

24 You are a newspaper reporter and you write about books and TV programmes. Write a report about 'Face the Raven' for your readers. Should they buy this book? Why (not)?

25 Explain why 'Face the Raven' is a good example of a science fiction story.

26 Peter Capaldi was very successful as the twelfth Doctor on British television. Imagine that there will be a new Doctor soon. You are the person who will choose the actor. Who do you want to see as the next Doctor? Explain your reasons.

27 Imagine that the present Doctor is looking for a new companion. Write to the Doctor. (*Dear Doctor* ...) Explain why you are the perfect person for this job.

28 You are a magazine writer. You have a meeting with Sarah Dollard, the writer of 'Face the Raven.' Make a list of questions to ask Ms Dollard about her work.

29 You are part of a science-fiction writing team. You have to think of four new types of aliens for a TV programme. Make a list of interesting names for your new aliens. Then describe them. What do they look like? What are they like? What can they do?

Answers for the Activities in this book are available from the Pearson English Readers website. A free Activity Worksheet is also available from the website. Activity worksheets are part of the Pearson English Readers Teacher Support Programme, which also includes Progress tests and Graded Reader Guidelines.

For more information, please visit:
www.pearsonenglishreaders.com

Word List

alarm (n) something that tells you of danger. If you are **alarmed**, you are worried or afraid.

alien (n) a fictional being from another world.

asylum (n) the right to stay in a safe place – in another country, for example. You ask for asylum to escape danger at home.

bracelet (n) something that you wear around your wrist.

cage (n) a place in which animals are kept safely.

contract (n) a written agreement between two people or companies.

diary (n) a book in which you write about your daily life.

graffiti (n) words or pictures that are painted on walls. Graffiti artists are usually breaking the law.

guilty (adj) who has done something wrong. If you are guilty of a crime, a judge can punish you.

hood (n) the part of a jacket or coat that covers your head. A **hoodie** is a jacket with a hood.

human (n/adj) a person from Earth. An **inhuman** person acts very unkindly towards other people.

immortal (adj) able to live for all time and never die.

knowledge (n) what is known about a subject.

lead (v) to walk in front of other people. A leader is the most important person in a group, with followers who listen to him/her.

mayor (n) the most important government officer in a town or city.

peaceful (adj) calm, without fighting.

raven (n) a large black bird.

revenge (n) an angry act against someone who has hurt you.

tattoo (n) a picture or words that are drawn on your body.

worm (n) a small animal with a long soft body and no legs that lives in earth.